# The Fine Art of Writing the Next Best Seller on Kindle

*By Omar Johnson*

I0421879

# Table of Contents

# Introduction

Amazon and its tiny little gadget the Kindle has totally galvanized and revolutionized the entire publishing industry. No longer do authors have to be at the mercy of the big publishing houses like Simon and Schuster, Random House, Harper Collins etc. to get their books out to the masses. The Kindle and Amazon's Kindle Direct Publishing program a platform that enables authors to self publish their books and make them available to a worldwide audience has totally disrupted an entire industry that needed to be disrupted like the music industry was when Apple introduced the IPod and the ITunes music store.

Traditionally, the only way to publish and get a book into the bookstores was to seek out a well connected literary agent who for a 10%-15% cut of the proceeds would shop a book around to the aforementioned publishers with the hopes of landing a book deal. For most authors flat-out rejection was normally the end result of this process. Those who weren't fortunate enough to be selected by the big name publishers were left out in the cold and their dreams of publishing and sharing their book with the world quickly became a distant faded fantasy.

Then Amazon came along and changed the game. Authors were now able to publish their books in an e-book format and have it distributed digitally throughout the world. Of course e-books have been around even before Amazon decided to get into the e-book market. However, never before have e-books had access to a platform like Amazon with a customer base of 300 million buyers who have their credit cards on file and are ready to instantly make a purchase with one click of the mouse.

The opportunities are tremendous for you as an author and Amazon doesn't mind sharing with you a big chunk of the pie. Never in the history of publishing until now have authors had a chance to get paid a 70% royalty rate for every book that they sell while maintaining full ownership of their published work.

The bottom line is, Amazon has set the stage for you as an author to make a boatload of cash by publishing your book on the Kindle and the only thing that you have to do is know how to effectively write a book that will catapult you to Kindle book stardom.

So how do you exactly write a book like that? What are the secrets? This is what this book in detail will show you, The Fine Art of Writing the Next Best Seller on Kindle. So without further ado let's dive in. Shall we?

# Chapter I: Most Popular Content in EBooks/ Personal Branding

Utilizing Kindle it is possible to write a book about anything, however, to increase the chances of success as a writer, the first thing I might want to ask myself is what has been selling? Are there ways I could take my idea for a book and incorporate the winning ideas which have been selling on the market into my work? Does a book have to be purely one category or style in order to sell? Or can it utilize different elements which make up multiple parts of a book?

The answer is very simple, it is best to write what has been successful, and pick up different elements. The most popular books borrow from different books and create themselves as a hybrid mix of popular categories incorporating the best elements from each category.

What are the most popular categories currently for eBooks on Kindle? The categories are as different as the authors who wrote them. In the list of the top 100 e books that were published in 2012 three of them were made into movies in 2012. Books such as *Beautiful Creatures and The Silver Linings Playbook* have been on the list of the top 100 e-books for more than 52 weeks.

Hollywood is also looking now among the ranks of the top 10 lists on Kindle to find their next most popular screenplays and movies. To Hollywood these books are a shoe in since they have already at that point established their audiences. Hollywood much like traditional publishers utilizes the same formula to decide what it is that they are going to produce and many classic stories which have always turned a profit are being rereleased with a new twist simply for their profitability.

Many of these titles include a retelling of fairy tales, or a complete remake of a classic film. New e-books such as *The Silver Linings Playbook* allow for authors to change the face of Hollywood one book at a time with suggesting to them through book sales that it is possible to in fact remake the list of selling formulas through book sales.

**Paranormal Romance**, books such as Beautiful Creatures and the Vampire Diaries have taken off in ways that it is hard to imagine their authors could think of at the time. For example, the Vampire Diaries when it was first published in 1993 was popular in teen circles and talked about among friends. However, L.J. Smith could not have imagined back then that it would in fact be turned into a full-fledged television show at that time.

Beautiful Creatures is the first of 4 books and is being hailed as the New Twilight, as the movie is in production now. Beautiful Creatures alone has sold over one million copies on Kindle. When a contract for a movie is signed the average production time is only a year and a half.

Many new authors are out there right now trying their hands at penning the next best paranormal romance. The category has showed its universal appeal as it frees the reader from the constraints of everyday reality by removing the elements of time, space, reality, and the physical universe. In this respect the reader is able to find themselves swept away into a world of fantasy and romance. This category is the ultimate first class ticket to a world of imagination where bills, screaming bosses, and other issues have no hold on the reader.

**Erotica** still thought of by some traditional publishers as taboo it is quickly becoming one of the most popular categories on Kindle. Many readers who would have been embarrassed to climb into the First Class seat on an airplane reading an erotica book are now able to sit down and read the book electronically without having to worry what the person who is sitting next to them is going to think about the topic.

E.L. James has easily proven the chops of this category with 50 Shades of Grey which started off as fan fiction for Twilight readers. Now E.L. James is projected with the first book in her series alone, and the upcoming movie to have outsold J.K. Rowling and be well on her way to surpassing the Harry Potter franchise. There is a book on Kindle for any desire and any taste.

**Business Books**. Have you ever thought of a concept for a business book from an organization you worked for, ever thought of how it should have been employed and things should have been executed? This may be the perfect time to get it down on paper. Right now more than ever many business books are taking off in new ways with new and simpler concepts.

Figurative books as well such as *Who Moved My Cheese,* have also taken hold on Kindle, as it is very easy for organizations to pass smaller books to their workers who can utilize the metaphors and easily consume the content.

### Personal Branding

These days a lot of business people talk about it but there is not a lot of detail about what it is exactly. You as an author need to have a brand, a set of concepts and objectives which you believe in and represent yourself to be. When you are writing you are building that brand for your audience, it is as consumable for them as your books. If you are a romance writer for example your audience is actively building an image in their heads of who you are and how you live.

In the past the image of the author was controlled by the publisher, this is a huge part of your brand. These days it is a relationship which is owned by the author in the world of self-publishing, and the readers get to directly connect to you without any third party interference or any barriers. As a self-published author there are many things you need to take into consideration.

What are you willing to share with your readers? What parts of yourself are you willing to share?

For example one way that you can connect directly with your readers is by starting a Facebook page for your book. Then you can suggest the page to friends and get the word out. If you decide that you would still like to have more followers for your page on Facebook you can also start a Facebook ad campaign which is custom designed to the needs of the creator.

With all the tools of technology available to the author it is amazing what can be produced on a small dime. With an advertising campaign on a shoe string budget of just $30 a week it is possible to generate ads with over 300 likes. And when this happens other people begin to talk about your page amongst their friends.

Facebook will also send you a customized report of how many clicks you are generating per week and how many people are seeing your ad; also it is possible to update your ad midstream in a campaign. This means that you can add new content to your advertisement, which the Facebook staff will then approve within a matter of hours. With new content constantly in your ad you are able to reach new readers who will be interested in your content.

With a Facebook page for your book and one for yourself as an author you are able to share daily progress about yourself as an author and any new milestones which you reach with your book. People inherently want to have a part in that, with a Facebook page they are able to follow your progress step by step and feel like they are actively contributing to the progress by following you and talking about it with their friends.

Constant updates to both pages are necessary, at a minimum on a daily basis and if possible much more to ensure that readers have the most current content. If you do not have any content to share which is related to your book, share something which is related to the subject matter. If you are writing a book about werewolves, share folklore about werewolves to ensure that your readers are constantly entertained. This can be other content from the internet and does not have to be directly from your site.

Your blog. Yes it is necessary to have a blog, if you write under your real name and also write under a pen name it is necessary to have two. Think of small little things to write about such as what gives you inspiration, your personal reading list, updates about where you are going with your work. All of these little things will keep your readers hungering for more as you update them. It is small little personal touches which keep a reader coming back for more so that they can learn as much as possible about the author.

YouTube. Create a YouTube channel about your book and your work, discuss what the motivation was for you to write your book.  Explain the story behind your book to your fans, and tell them about the characters in the book or about your area of expertise.  As you move forward with other pursuits you are more marketable with a following and a fan base to prospective agents.

As well, there is no more personal a way for your fans to be able to interact with you than by seeing you even in your home in front of your own web cam discussing your book with them.  This will build a relationship with the readers that publishers would die to have because it takes out the middle man and allows you to reach the readers directly.

Your Brand.  When we talk about the brand, we are talking about an image, a presence, an email template even.  Take the time to understand the intricacies of your email platform, develop a template that is inherently yours.  When you are talking to perspective agents, producers, writers, etc. you want to ensure that you have an email which will stand out from your competitors and from other authors.

Your brand image must be consistent across the board so people understand who you are and the image you are projecting.  Brand schizophrenia is one of the worst issues that a writer can have, for example, portraying yourself as an erotica writer and as a children's book writer can be a bit confusing for readers, agents, and anyone doing a simple Google search.  That is the beauty of brand consistency, and also the need for a pen name rolled up in one simple sentence.

# Chapter II: Planning Your Niche in the Popular Market

So you have decided to write that book finally…what book that is on the top sellers list is it like? That needs to be your first question, look at other books in the category you are writing in and see what has worked for them and what hasn't. Are there 1000 books which have tried to copy the formula which E.L. James utilized? If so following in her exact footsteps will not be the way to go.

Although it has worked for her, she was the first to come up with this blue print, for this reason it worked. With the thousands of copycat writers out there however, if you use the same aspects of her writing you will find yourself one in a herd of authors trying to be a part of the same plan. This will not work for you.

The "Look Inside" this book feature that Amazon offers on its site is a wonderful tool that you should use to your advantage. It allows you to "Look Inside" books which are similar to yours and read some of the content. You can browse the table of contents, you can see the chapters and content, and see what else is out there.

Research is part of any authors due diligence, when you pitch a nonfiction book to a publisher they ask you specifically to write a book proposal. Part of that proposal involves finding other writers who are similar to you, why your book is different, and what your marketing plan is for the book.

Large publishers will spend some money in the realm of marketing, but a lot of the time this is left up to the author as well. The publisher believes that an author must have skin in the game and for this reason they usually do not cover the cost of all marketing. However, if you are a self-published author, marketing your own book will be more important than ever. For this reason homework and due diligence are merely a step in the road to becoming a best-selling Kindle author.

### Step 1: Research your competition.

Isolate the elements that the other author has used to make their work stand out. Is it for example a lot of credible research and charts to back up their viewpoint? Is it memorable characters and awesome plot development? The key element is to find what they have used that has been popular and sold and to completely customize this for your own use.

### Step 2: Find winning elements.

Just as you will find the winning elements in a manuscript there are always things which could have been done better. For example, should a chapter have had more research on a particular topic? Could a character have been just a little more juicy with a few more paragraphs of description?

If you really want to do your due diligence, buy a hard copy of the book and mark the manuscript with flaws and accolades. This way as you are creating your own book you are able to reference the manuscript as many times as you want to see the way a particular author handled a situation. Do not hesitate to write in books, I remember as a child I was always told never to write in books, when I look back now I find that some of the best ideas I ever generated were in the margins of texts while I was reading them. Remember, the whole reason you bought a hard copy was to learn, so treat it like a textbook blueprint for your book.

### Step 3: Find weaknesses in other's texts.

Now that you know what works and what does not it is time to form a blue print for your books. As Aristotle said, you cannot understand a whole without understanding the sum of its parts. For this reason, you must draw up an outline which will become your beginning blue print for the book.

Do not concern yourself with whether or not this is going to be a fiction or a non-fiction book, the whole point at this moment in time is to merely get your ideas and your words down on paper so they can be edited and tweaked as you move along in the process. This is merely a skeleton to begin in the process of building the book.

### Step 4: Start an outline

Remember as well that starting an outline does not mean that you are committed to its contents 100%. As you write and as you move along you will find that your style will change, and with those changes in style and content your outline will also be modified. Part of creating anything is realizing that until it is sent to press it is a Work In Progress, and that means that it can be modified at any time.

## Here is a short Checklist:

**Step 1: Research your competition.**

**Step 2: Find winning elements.**

**Step 3: Find weaknesses in other's texts.**

**Step 4: Start an outline**

# Chapter III: Fiction vs. Non Fiction Navigating the Waters with Precision

So now there is a skeleton for the body which is about to be built, the outline for your book. Before you begin fleshing out the idea it is very important to begin firstly by understanding what the difference is between fiction and non-fiction.

As simple as that sounds there are sometimes places where there can be a lot of grey area. For example, you are writing a historical novel where the people in the book are drawn on inspiration from true people. Or maybe you are writing a book that is a true crime story, how do you categorize a book that is based on true events and you need to change the names to protect the innocent? These are a few examples of grey that need to be covered and addressed as well as making certain that you have the write elements for your book.

When you are writing fiction, the world is more or less your oyster as you are able to create any elements you would like without the constraints of reality, time and space. However, it is important when you are creating to make certain that you are not plagiarizing someone else's work unintentionally.

Maybe, you are utilizing a character that you like from another book as your own without introducing enough new elements of development to make that character your own. Are you possibly using someone else's setting without developing it to make it your own? As valuable as money in the bank is to people, ideas are the same for writers'. For this reason make sure you develop your own ideas, and your own characters, if they are loosely based on someone else's you must invest more time in planning.

There are basic elements which must be utilized when writing a fiction manuscript:

## Elements of a Fiction Manuscript:

**Plot:** This is the story and what you are planning to have happen. As you are thinking about the plot and the story line, imagine your book as a movie. What elements would make your book more intriguing here? Plan the entire plot out ahead if possible, as an outline of the chapters. Within your total book outline form a basic list of what will happen in each chapter.

## Example: Jack and Jill

**Chapter 1: Jack and Jill Go Up a Hill For Water**
**Chapter 2: Jack Falls Down**
**Chapter 3: Jack Breaks His Crown**
**Chapter 4: Jill Comes Tumbling After**
**Chapter 5: No One Got Water….**
**Chapter 6: What Happens Next?**

**Setting:** Where is the story happening? This element is one of the most important parts of a book. The reader must be able to picture themselves in this location, for this reason it is important that the author write about a location which they have knowledge of or have experienced.

If it is a completely fictional location the author must imagine that they are in fact an artist painting every scene for the reader. The reader needs to know about the weather, how sunrises look, and the noises which are present in the atmosphere at night. It is important that the reader is able to imagine every element of the place. If it is completely a new universe the author must also explain the laws of reality as they apply to the new location.

**Character:** Who is the main character? What is their background specifically? If your readers know everything about the main characters you are writing about then they will be able to identify with aspects of the character's personality. Each reader must see themselves through the eyes of the main character, this way they are able to identify with the character and form a sense of identification with the character.

Describe the way a character thinks, walks, and make certain to allow the reader to see the interior monologue of the character. If possible give the character an accent, or a catchphrase which will make the reader know more about the character. If the story takes place in the south, study the dialogue and the attributes of southern dialect. Deploy small little pieces of information about the character at key points in the manuscript, give away just enough information that the reader is dying for more.

**Conflict:** Every good book has a driving conflict. As in what is being solved by reading this book for the character? Has the main character become a vampire, is trying to overcome cancer, is learning how to speak Spanish while living in the country?

Whatever the main conflict is in the story it must be developed in great detail for the characters. The route that the main character is going to take should also be clear to the reader from the intonations internally that the character is making. Will this be an internal struggle or an external struggle and what are the elements which can be added to make the struggle greater?

Is it a familial conflict which is causing stress for all parties involved as they try to find their way through the situation, a battle between dueling lovers maybe? The reader must be so involved in the conflict that they think about it when walking away from the book. Also if you are thinking about having this made into a television show or a movie everything will be about conflict.

**Symbol:** A symbol is something which will represent other items in the book. If this is a vampire novel the color red could be used throughout to give the color of blood. Small elements like a red rose, or a particular reference to feathers. The idea is to pick one overarching image which can be used and can become a theme throughout the rest of the text. The next time your reader encounters a red rose if that is your symbol, while shopping at the local market the first thing which will come to mind will in fact be the book and the plot.

**Point of View:** How are you going to tell the story? Are you telling it in the third person like you are writing a text book, from the second person using you? Or are you telling the story from the first person with the utilization of the word I? It is important to decide this from the beginning of the story as you do not want to swap perspectives throughout the course of the text. You will drive editors and readers crazy.

**Theme:** This is the main thought and the main feeling you are leaving behind at the conclusion of the story. When the reader thinks back on the story that you told, this will in fact be the last statement that the reader is left. It is important to make certain that the theme of the work is clear in your mind from the beginning. In this way as the content is developed with the theme in mind instead of realizing that something was done off track and having to return and rewrite a section.

Now that you have a diagram for the beginning there is a rough outline, sit down and write up a blue print for your fiction book. Again this is the beginning roadmap that will continue to grow and develop as different elements are added to the plot and story. But this is a good place to start. Room is being left between the paragraphs to add your thoughts. Ask yourself:

What is my **plotline**? What is going to happen in the story?

Where is the **setting**? Where is the story taking place, what is my knowledge of the place? Do I need more knowledge of the place?

Who is my main **character**? Where is he/she from? What do they look like, what are their likes and dislikes? Does this person have a lover, what is their orientation, what music does he/she like? All of these little elements when thought out in advance will add spice as well as believability to your character.

Do you know someone you could interview from this corner of the world. For example, if your character is Russian, do you know someone from the same area of Russia who would be willing to give you a snapshot of life from his/her perspective?

**Conflict:** What is the main conflict of the story? If it is a person with cancer, do you know someone who has undergone this situation who would be willing to give you access to his thoughts and emotions? Do research into historical figures who have had similar situations to the character that you are writing about and find out how that person dealt with the issue.

What **symbols** are you going to use? What other authors have written about the same subject matter you are utilizing? What symbols have they used in their work to describe the situation? What is the historical significance behind the symbol?

For example, has it ever been a part of the lore of another culture? How can you play off of that association in your own text and add in small references to the symbols historical context? That historical association can add an element of universalism to the text which will transcend cultures.

What is your **Point of View**? Why have you chosen to write in the tense, and point of view you have? Is it because it comes naturally given the subject matter?

Develop your thoughts as to why and how this is going to benefit your audience.

What is the **theme**?  Where are your ideas about the theme of the book coming from?  Is this something that is coming from other works like yours?  What worked for them?  And specifically, when people think of your work what is the key takeaway message you want them to have?

Hopefully now you feel comfortable to get started with planning the content of your fiction book.  Remember that any of this can be modified along the way and until the book is published all of this is merely a work in progress.

While writing fiction allows the mind to wander and to imagine, writing nonfiction creates an entire other set of objectives.  The goal of the writer is either to provide information, relive an experience, or report information much in the way that a journalist would.

The first step of writing any nonfiction book is to determine the purpose of the book.  What is it in fact that you are trying to do, if you are writing a book about Elizabeth I, your objective would be to report all of the events exactly as they happened.

If you are in fact writing something like a true crime book, you would be recalling the experience as it happened as well, from the memory of the person telling the story. As mentioned previously this is one of those areas where grey area can become an issue.

Can you change the names of the people involved in a true crime incident and still have it as a nonfiction book? The answer here is absolutely, the beginning of the book must simply contain a statement which mentions that the names have been changed to protect the innocent. So now here are the elements which must be considered to plan an amazing nonfiction book.

## Elements of a Non Fiction Book

**Outlining.** Since you started your book production you have been planning an outline. Now it is time to take those chapters that you have and put flesh on the bones. At the beginning of the outline look at your chapter titles. Underneath each one of these chapter headings place at least 5 items which are going to be included in the chapter. These items in the outline should be a mix of historical facts, items you wish to cover and small pieces of information from the story which will add to the credibility and interest level of the manuscript.

Looking deeper into this that should mean that the historical facts are what actually happened and the sequence of time is accurate when reporting facts. The pieces you want to cover should be smaller elements of the story which will add to the character development of the characters. And finally the last interesting facts should be pieces of information about the main subject, or odd facts to draw your reader in.

**Research** is the most important step in the Non Fiction writing process. As you are beginning to plan your outline and add detail into the outline, there is nothing more important than to conduct the most thorough research possible into your subject. Research all the books which you can find on the subject, cross check books to see if the authors have the same opinions. If it is a current topic check all of the local newspapers which might have reported on the subject. Check to see if the newspaper's report any key witnesses with contact information you might be able to contact for an inside perspective into the matter.

Doing a personal interview with a person who might have been involved in the case will add credibility as well as give you an amazing insight into the psychology of the case. By having a first person insight into the case you will be able to vicariously relive all of the experiences of the situation.

You will be able to see all of the little details that the interviewee recalls including the sights, smells, feelings and appearances. This is by far the second best thing other than experiencing the event yourself.

Cross reference your files and your information. Make certain that at the end of the day the information that you have compiled is the most factual, detailed, and accurate. Try to avoid he said she said information from conflicting sources.

**Character** development, just like in a fiction book it is important to develop the characters with as much details as possible in a nonfiction book. In the same way that the characters can enchant and inspire in the fiction books, in non-fiction attention to detail is key to portray the accuracy of the situation.

Little items should be looked into such as if the protagonist had a lisp, the way the character wore his/her hair and dressed. Do not tell the story in generalities but get into the deepest details of the person and try to tell the story as if you were going to write an essay on the non-fiction character's soul. All of those little details are again the window into the past so that the reader is able to envision themselves there and be a part of the conversation.

**Dialogue** development is mission critical as well for creating an accurate nonfiction manuscript. As many nonfiction narrative books have proven over the years, accurate dialogue can make or break the success of a book. By trying to recreate what was actually said in the past you will give insight into the story and also buy the credibility of the readers as they see the way things actually happened.

One thing that has been the challenge of history has been for the historians to accurately record conversations which were held along the sides of battle lines across the sand of time. When reporting a nonfiction event it is these moments which must be carefully recorded and dictated in the manuscript for posterity.

There are a few other elements we should consider here with nonfiction as well and reporting. What are the good elements of reporting, we must harken to our press hats. They are the famous Who, What, When, Why, and How, longingly known as the 4w's and the H. These are also the chronic elements that for an accurate story must be told;

**Who:** This specifically outlines who was involved in a particular situation, their history, background, defining characteristics and every possible statistic. The people involved in the story must be considered in complete detail when researching and then when planning their development. One key point would be to make certain that you have covered all of the details of character development.

**What:** What is it that happened, what is the story you are telling? Make certain that you write all of the details and take the events from all perspectives that were involved. One easy way to do this is to make a full outline of all of the events in sequential order. After that another important step is to list all of the items and also the different points of thought in the outline and the names of the differing parties.

**When:** When did it happen? As you are taking notes and planning this element of the text, look into the details of the times. This as an author will help you to create the most believable environment, what were the clothing fads? What was the popular music, who was running the country? What were the political issues of the time, world issues, and local issues? Are there any other factors here which are not covered that might be relevant to the time period of the story? Are there any particular elements which might have to do with the time that pertain to the who, or the character in question?

**Why:** The next question is why did this happen? How was it culturally significant? What kind of impact did this event have on the community, the country and the world? What is the key takeaway from all of the information to describe how things are changing now and how it is relevant now?

**How:** How did things transpire? What took place? How did the situation start? How did the situation end? And how could a situation like that be prevented from happening again, or how could a good thing like that happen again? Is it possible that the situation could in fact be recreated?

Remember when covering these areas to think like a journalist and as Paul Harvey always comments, get "the rest of the story." Many times when manuscripts are written they are only written from one perspective and sometimes the opposite point of view, other characters involved, or even complete historical facts which might have been game changers have been completely deleted or ignored form the manuscripts.

In order to offer a round and full perspective the interests of all parties must be represented and must be present. Nonfiction is about truthfulness, accuracy, and fairness to all.

Armed with these tools you are well on your way to navigating the waters between fiction and non-fiction and thereby starting an amazing piece of art. Using the fundamental elements of success outlined here you will develop the manuscript to its highest level of potential.

## Chapter IV: Creating a Title that Sells

Your book's title will be ultimately its calling card. It is very important that it is memorable, fresh and catchy. With tons of books being uploaded to Kindle every day, it is extremely important to ensure that yours is memorable. Since titles are not copyrighted and cannot be it is possible that someone else will have the same topic. And yet what is really important is the way we express ourselves in the title. The more uniquely the title is stated the more it will resonate with the reader, publisher and marketing opportunities.

Make certain that you are considering the kind of book you are writing when planning the title. Many non-fiction books do a poor job of distinguishing themselves from fiction, or even from self-help and business. The book title needs to be catchy, motivating and instant.

### Non Fiction Books

For Nonfiction books it is very important to ensure that the reader knows what the take away will be from their time investment. When the reader is finished, what will he have accomplished as a human being? It needs to be clear, it needs to be concise and to the point. Consider the nonfiction book an objective statement that the reader is using to evaluate the value and content of the book. You could write the most amazing book in the world but without a great title no one will take it home and at the end of the day the gem could be hiding in between the pages.

Nonfiction books are also very much like extended thesis statements and for this reason they may need to have subtitles. The subtitle is a longer explanation of the mission statement and the intent of the book.

**A Few Great Examples Include:**

*Who Moved My Cheese: An Amazing Way to Deal with Change in Your Work and in Your Life*

**Rich Dad Poor Dad: What The Rich Teach Their Kids About Money That the Poor and Middle Class Do Not!**

Narrative nonfiction and also memoirs utilize a different art form of crafting a title, the reader is given the promise of a compelling story in the pages. For this reason it is also very important here to provide an awesome, smoldering and catchy title. The title should be something that says something about the Memoir, was there a compelling moment, a catchy phrase, something that can encapsulate the total story in just a few words? This is the content that should make up the title.

Celebrity biographies and historical biographies should have all of the flash and circumstance that is a part of the lives as they were lived. For example, they should say something about the historical figure or celebrity and point to a personality trait or maybe to a part of their lives.  A few great examples include:

*My Horizontal Life* by Chelsea Handler

*George Washington: The Indispensable Man*

Both of these titles give the reader a very clear idea of the content of the books and are also catchy, entertaining, and fun.

## Fiction Books

The titles of fiction books should be a sneak peek into the content of the story, so for example a catchy phrase which hints at the story.  *Fifty Shades of Grey* is an excellent title for E.L. James' book because it hints at the greyness of human sexuality and at the potential for differing areas of opinion on the BDSM situation she writes about.  Also titles which are inflammatory will catch the attention of readers who will feel that they have to know more at the very moment when they are seeing the title, their response will be to buy a book.

## Key Title Takeaways:

1. **Make it Catchy**
2. **Make sure it Reflects your Book**
3. **It is a Huge Marketing Tool**
4. **Write multiple Options to Make Sure you Choose the Right Option**

5.  **Know if Eventually You Undergo a Republishing in a Traditional Publishing House Titles May Be Altered By Editors and Agents.**
6.  **Think About the Core of Your Message in the Title.**

## Chapter V: Creating a Winning Cover

So you have written a book, where are you going to get a cover? What even makes a good cover to begin with? Unless you are a natural as an artist, most writers aren't, which is why we use computers, it is difficult to know where to start and also how to get there. What elements do successful book covers have in them and how do you as a writer, not an artist, replicate that success?

**Things that must be considered when designing a cover are very simple:**

1.  **How do you promise to inspire, motivate, change someone's life and make it amazing?** You sell them a vision by the art on the front of your cover, it might be that it is a beautiful woman sitting on a tranquil beach, or it might be a gorgeous moonlit night. The consumer is shopping with their dollars wanting to buy the vision that you are selling. As authors sometimes we forget that we are in fact selling, we are selling

our craft, ourselves, and the fantasy that comes with our personal brand.

2. **Make the reader want to know more about the cover, for example, why do you think that romance novels are so popular?** It is because the covers border on scandalous, there is the gorgeous woman with a burgeoning bosom and also the man with his hair flying in the wind. All of these covers reflect the fantasy that the reader wants to have as a part of their experience.

3. **Get a well-crafted book cover, which is beautiful, inspirational and meaningful. DO NOT insult your readers with a poorly designed cover.** The cover is one of the largest success factors of a book. If it is not beautiful and inspirational when someone sees it they will pass over the book simply because it was not attention grabbing enough. The graphic images on the front of the book need to make the reader want to pick up the book and open it. If your book cover looks like it was made out of construction paper it will not be acceptable to anyone, mainly the reader and it will interfere with the sales you are trying to accomplish.

So we have established what works and what doesn't work. But here is one of the most important points, if you are not an artist how do you design your own cover?  There are a few different schools of thought here and a few different options.

You could draw your own abstract cover for the front of the book utilizing your own talents if this is done however it is important to know that you will not be able to use the original piece of art.  You will need to get a great digital camera and be prepared to take lots of photos of the art.  Also you are going to require different kinds of cover designs. So for example you may need to provide a .png file for some, a jpeg for others, and finally a pdf for some others.

In addition to having these different kinds of files on hand it is also important to know that different formats will also require different sizes of photos. For example, this also means you must be familiar with resizing images in many different programs and formats.  Most PCs will come with a resizing tool like Microsoft Photo Editor or Paint.

However, if you are not a master at software like this what is there that you can do to increase your ability to manipulate and change images?  There are quite a few free programs out there like Gimp which allow the user to do some amazing things with images.

However, one thing about the free programs is that they are not necessarily the most user friendly programs. It behooves the writer to download the guide and to plan to spend a lot of time reading it and figuring out the intricacies of the software. This means that the most popular effects will be slightly difficult to master. Upon logging into Gimp the first time the user will be slightly surprised at the number of options and the number of buttons.

If you are not a designer and have never used a program like this before a few things to consider are key terms which are universally applied to programs like this across the board.

### Gimp:

**Alignment:** This indicates if the photo should be left justified, right justified, or center justified. If it is left it will be to the left hand side of the page, right will be to the right side and center will happen in the middle of the page.

**Size:** This indicates the size of the image and whether it should be changed and manipulated. Kindle e-books utilize a maximum amount of pixels for a concentrated image. For this reason the images will be bright and will show great detail. When modifying a photo you can choose to re-size it either by pixels or size by selecting the radio option.

For a proper Kindle format the image must be adjusted not by the size option but by the pixel option. For best quality on the Kindle, your cover art image should be 1563 pixels on the shortest side and 2500 pixels on the longest side. The Kindle platform will have a maximum of the size of file that it is in fact able to withstand and upload. For this reason please take this into initial planning when designing the cover.

Resizing a photo by size and not pixels is also known as Scaling. Gimp is utilized by many a starving artist as it does not cost anything whereas a competitor like Photoshop can costs many thousands of dollars and Gimp has all of the same effects and features.

**Masking:** It is also possible to use this feature to add and or delete certain features from the existing frames in a photo. Maybe you only want to show a particular part of a feature, you are able here to utilize Masking and to cover the part that should not be seen. It could be a brand, a logo, someone's personal information or any aspect of a photo that must be changed.

**Transparency:** In Gimp transparency there is an option which allows the user to change the degree of the background image for clarity and sharpness depicted. The background image may be either slightly blurry, clear, or transparent. The user is able to determine the graininess of the photo by using this feature. Different levels of transparency can change the old time or historical attributes of the photo.

**Layering:** You have the ability to Layer images as well in Gimp by utilizing their Layer feature. This essentially means that you can stack multiple images, up to 5 on top of one another in order to be able to choose how you want the main cover to look.

**Zooming:** Like any other software, zooming allows you to go into a tiny area of the cover and to make essential changes to the cover to ensure that it is perfect and is error free. Sometimes with a photo of a real or live piece of art, there can be little details that may not be seen until zooming in very closely, these might include wanting to smooth out lumps of dried paint, removing the signature of the artist who painted the piece etc. All of these are possible to see and to remove and tweak with the aid of the zoom feature.

**Transform:** This feature will allow you to flip the image and even has a very interesting Random Assignment feature for an image. In case you are feeling more inspired and less planned you might be able to utilize this feature with multiple images to add spice to the alignment of the cover.

**Filters:** There are many filters which are sorting options for features, some are very advanced like inserting animation into a photo and others are still very basic. However in the toolbar itself you will find roughly about 50 options for the filters.

Gimp is easy to use once the author gets the hang of it, but prior to starting any book cover project it is very important that the author reads all of the guides for Gimp. Having not done this myself once I was amazed at how quickly it is to become frustrated with all of the bells and whistles. Something as simple as opening a file for modification can be slightly daunting, as the old saying goes when in doubt read the directions.

### Microsoft Paint

This is a simple program and a very easy one to use. If your mind is on overload when you open up a program and you only want to see two tabs then this is a great program for you. In the File tab you will find all of the similar commands that you have seen in the past in the Word format, PowerPoint format, Excel and every other format. For this reason it is a nice standby. The second tab contains all of the features and changes that need to be had to manipulate the images.

**Resize:** Here you are able to choose the size of the photo and the changes which need to be made. You can either change the photo by Scaling or by Pixels. After this resizing make sure that you save the results of your changes. One wise thing you might want to do is to create a folder on your computer for each project you are working on and then put all of the book cover revisions in that folder.

Conversely, there can be an issue when you are making multiple revisions of the photo because you might not be sure where you are putting all of the different revisions. When you need to reference a file and convert it back and forth from format to format you need to know where everything is at that moment and have it at the end of your fingertips.

**Shape Selector:** This feature allows you to square and to choose different shapes to insert into your photo.

**Fill:** Allows you to paint inside a shape or to paint inside a background for the cover.

**Text:** Here you are able to choose the font and the size of the font to put lettering on the front of the book. All of the same fonts, sizes, and features are available just as in Word and in the same locations. Also here you are able to change the color of the text. Make certain that the text color does not interfere with the background of the book specifically. So for example, if you have dark backgrounds make sure that you choose a darker background for the text.

Text formats should be bright and bold, wide fonts without crazy characters so that the person who is approaching the book from far away is clearly able to read the title and also read the name of the author on the cover without losing themselves in the background. The easiest way to do this is to use fonts like Times New Roman or Arial Bold.

When utilizing fonts which are curvy it becomes difficult for readers to read from far away, it also makes it more work on the brain to remember the title because of the curvature of the letters. This is why it is easier for the mind to process information which is printed, versus the information which is written in cursive.

### Snag It

Another program which is typically installed on all computers and is very helpful for writers is Snag it. It allows for the author to grab copies of a photo or of a desktop and save that image and utilize it for different formats. It automatically saves itself as a.png file and yet can be modified easily for use in the aforementioned programs.

Make certain that you know how to use the basic formats of Snag It in order to be able to take screenshots, and to save different kinds of images so that you will be able to implement it to add great drawings to your work.

### File Save As

If you are trying to save a file in a different format for example jpeg, .png, .rtf, .tif and are not sure what to do, open the file you have and copy the image, then copy the image to a Word document and use the File option and select Save As. After using this option you will be able to choose the format output you need.

## Different Sources of Covers:

1. **Do It Yourself:** As discussed earlier you can create your own cover by your own drawing or your own painting.

2. **Professional Cover Designers:** These are available for a small fee starting with around $50 for a stock image cover with no royalties or can also be custom designed on a book by book basis starting at around $150 and going up to $ 800 USD. When an artist designs a cover it is very important that they sign a Nondisclosure agreement (NDA) if they are working for hire stating that they will contribute to the book but are not seeking royalties.

What is the difference between flat fee and royalties? Here one thing to remember and consider is if you pay a writer a flat fee for their work they should not expect royalties when the book is published. However, once the book begins to take off sometimes this is not clear if it is not stated on paper in a format like an NDA.

3. **Deposit Photos:** A website like deposit photos, photo bucket etc. offer royalty free photos which

can be purchased and then have the information required added to them. This means that a photo can be sold to the author or artist with no royalties due to the site and no royalties due long term in sales. This means that outright the author has bought the rights by paying for the image or by buying the image through a subscription plan.

A subscription plan is a great idea if you are using massive amounts of content. Maybe you are using stock photos for a book you are working on or have multiple projects; all of this can be accomplished easily with a subscription plan.

4. **Friend's Art:** Using a friend's art for your book cover is a great way to help them with exposure. However, one thing to consider is you need to have your friend sign an NDA and agree on the terms way before the final cover is designed, uploaded and used.

Hopefully after this chapter, you feel better, more in charge and have a direction of where to go. Here are a few other things to think about when planning the image.

1. **The cover is as important as the title: make it memorable, gorgeous and approachable.**
2. **Decide how you are going to obtain a cover.**

3. Make certain to understand the intricacies of the source whether it is using technology or working with a friend.
4. Have fun, covers are the main touch point for the reader of the book. Even before they read the title, whatever image is chosen will stand out in the minds of the reader.

# Chapter VI: Plot Elements that Win You Big Sales

Best Selling books always have a few common elements which are represented in their pages. The story which is being told by the author is essentially that of the mythic hero in a universal tale being told over and over again but being adapted to a new time and cultural situation. We are going to discuss some of those elements right now…essentially it boils down to 10 winning elements. These elements transcend the writing genre as well and translate to media across the board, so if you have film ambitions for your story please pay attention.

**Element One: A Broken Family:** all great books have an element of a family which is broken in one sense or another. This might be due to an untimely death, a divorce, or an argument between brother and sister. Essentially the main element is that the home must have an issue or there is no reason for the main character to leave on a quest. If everything is perfect in paradise, or in the home base there is nothing to search for, on the part of the character.

**Element Two: Highly Emotionally Charged Characters:** If you think about Tony Soprano or Belle from the Red Shoe Diaries you will recognize one major element. They both have huge elements of his/her personality pulling against one another. Whether it is the guilt of being a prostitute or a gangster, both works are penned so that you see the interior machinations of the characters.

Even a character like Tony Soprano who would be the archetypal bad guy if the work were penned in a different way is now an understandable and likeable guy. The reason he is likeable is because it is possible to imagine him with the devil on one shoulder and the angel on the other shoulder, much like the old Warner Brother's cartoons.

**Element Three: "Us Versus Them":** This means that there is a clear divide in between both sides of a conflict, this can be Spartans versus Persians, Democrats versus Republicans or the Germans versus the Americans. The most important thing is that there is a conflict that is created between two opposing and polar sides which can never be mistaken for the opposite side, each entity is clearly defined.

This is apples against oranges, and cats against dogs. The writer's job is to ensure that both sides are shown in different respects and are not confused for one another. One side will generally be more sympathized with considering the perspective of the writer. However, the line in the sand will be clear and distinct.

**Element Four: Periods of Learning:** Whether it is a midlife crisis, a romantic sabbatical, or a quest to find oneself the main character must undergo a period of learning something. This is the story of personal growth of the main character. For this reason whatever the personal challenge, is the reader must be able to identify with the character or be able to picture someone that he/she knows as the character. For this reason the struggle or the learning period must be universal to ensure it appeals to readers.

**Element Five: Conspiracies**: Let's face it nothing gets society to question things like a good conspiracy. If it questions the norms or the trends of history an audience will listen. For this reason if you have an original conspiracy idea or one that has not been tapped into much, like the *Davinci Code* the piece is bound to take off. Simply by questioning the laws of accepted history and by calling Biblical theory into question it has earned itself a place at the table of best conspiracy movies.

**Element Six: A Twist:** During the plot there needs to be a small element which will lead the readers astray. This can be as small as a hint that the story may not turn out the way the reader wants it too or that there could be other possibilities. Keeping your reader guessing is an essential element of a successful book. Think of the twist as an alternate ending for your readers, you will keep them interested and coming back for more.

**Element Seven: Momentum:** The reason that suspense books sell at the rate they do is not because of careful plot development. However, it is because of the quick clip of the dialogue in the book that people continue to turn the page and see what happens next. One action leads into the next and into the next to ensure that the reader is so enveloped in the train of events that they forget about all other elements of the story.

If you are attempting to write a suspense novel, check out the masters such as John Grisham to see exactly how they draw in the reader and keep them with constant action and plot changes. Or a perusal of some great Sherlock Holmes classics will net you the same discoveries as you decide "who had done it?"

**Element Eight: An Awesome Villain:** The term awesome might be replaced with original, there needs to be a dialectical force of opposition which leads to the protagonist and the antagonist dancing in a beautiful tango of strife. A villain with all the right characteristics will leave the reader with one of two emotions, disgust or perhaps a sense of slight pity as the reader will feel that he or she can identify with the villain.

This is one of the key elements to building any story to its greatest extent, the villain may not be a person, and it could be a government entity, a monster, or an army. At the end of the day the most important factor is the emotional charge which the villain is able to elicit from the reader. Does the reader love him, hate him, and want him? As long as the reader remembers the villain and thinks about it when he walks away, the mission has been accomplished.

**Element Nine: Nostalgia:** We have all heard the sayings, "Life was simpler in the past," since the times of the Romans this has been a recurring theme in all of the books and movies which have pervaded our culture. People dream of living in the thirties or the forties with all the glamour and the glitter of Hollywood in its initial heyday.

However, they conveniently forget the elements of World War II and a Great Depression which were happening at that same time. Any great manuscript will have a hearkening to the past to return the reader to a simpler time and allow that nostalgia to come alive with fanciful settings and detailed descriptions.

**Element Ten: A Happy Ending:** As much as we might like not to think it, at the end of the day the reader wants a happy ending. Or at least minimally one which wraps the manuscript at a complete closure with satisfying results for the reader. In order for the reader to feel complete and satisfied the reader must know what happened to all of the interests and aspects of the characters that they cared about during the course of the manuscript. Those that are the hardest to digest are books which leave the reader hanging on the edge not knowing the fate of the hero or heroine.

An example of this would be in *Gone with the Wind* when Rhett Butler steps away from Scarlet and says, "Frankly my dear, I don't give a damn" and Scarlet resolves to get back her man. The audience was left hungering for more to the point of desperation, and 40 years after the author's death, another author took up Margret Mitchell's pen to try and complete the hanging conclusion.

Whether you are writing fiction or nonfiction the elements of storytelling are universal and the same across the board. The only difference here is that when writing nonfiction it is those tiny bits of unusual fact, gleaned from amazing research that paint the vibrant pictures of a complete and factual manuscript.

# Chapter VII: Issues with Style That Leave You Dead in the Water

As writers we are in fact human and flawed, as much as that seems impossible from time to time it is in fact part of life. For this reason we must accept that there are a lot of problems which are made in manuscripts, which are avoidable with careful correction.

Let's talk about 15 items which will leave your manuscript full of holes and lead to low sales. Consumers, even your average readers, will recognize quality. Much like a plumber would not leave a pipe leaking, a manuscript must also be free of holes. Sometimes however, as a writer it is hard to see the holes within your own manuscript. This checklist of items will assist in finding those issues.

**Issue 1: Lack of Development of Point of View:** So you are telling a story, how are you, the writer connected? Are you some distant third party observer who has never met anyone? Are you reading newspaper articles and trying to piece together a story without imagining you are the protagonist and thinking about all of the emotions of the situation? To say the least a piece in which there is a very distant point of view, the audience will not become engaged.

Whether the story is being told from the first or the second point of view it needs to be closely connected to the reader. How are they becoming a part of the story?

What elements have you not used to bring them into the space, and the time? Is it clear immediately to the reader what you are trying to accomplish by telling this story?

**Issue 2: Inadequate Character Feelings:** So we have a character but what are they feeling? Are they between a rock and a hard place financially, dying of a disease, stuck in the middle of unrequited love? All of these situations have very specific emotions which go along with them; the job of the author is to make the reader believe that the experience which is being recalled is one which the author has personally experienced.

What is meant by personally is that the level of character emotions and thoughts are believable. What we mean by believable is accurate to a person who has been in that situation. Not fabricated and forced on top of an uncomfortable book template, if you don't know what the appropriate thoughts and feels are for a person in a situation, interview someone who has been in the position of the character. Find out what his or her personal experience has been.

**Issue 3: An Opening Line Which Lacks Force:** The first line of a book is the most priceless. If the moment that the reader picks up the book and reads the first line of the book, he is not drawn into another world, or intrigued then the book will be set aside. In a world of constant distractions and immediate means of entertainment as close as your iPhone, the only way to keep the attention of your audience is to ensure that the words you use are engaging, memorable, and active.

Remember as a writer you are not only a content producer, but you are a word smith. What is the difference? A content producer merely writes content, the quality is not discussed. However, a wordsmith is able to take any phrase and turn a clever and enticing line. Be a wordsmith not a content producer, if success is in your cards!

**Issue 4: Unclear Goals of the Character:** One of the largest issues with writing is a lack of clear goals on the part of the character. When the story begins to develop it needs to be clear right out of the box to the reader what the mission is that the character is trying to achieve. Without this piece of information it is like leading the reader down a winding path with no point of conclusion.

**Issue 5: No Episodic Writing:** Every scene in a book should move the plot forward. The scene should not just tell you something about the character, but must in fact be written with purpose and with significance. For this reason as you are planning out your scenes make certain that you think about all of the elements of the plot whether the manuscript is fiction or nonfiction.

Each detail must move the plot forward and carry the reader down the path towards full unveiling and the plot twists. Again here think like a suspense writer and carry the reader down the path of the story.

**Issue 6: Grammar and Punctuation Issues:**
Believe it or not there are many manuscripts which make their way all the way to the printing presses still riddled with issues in grammar and punctuation. This means that the editing process has not been completed, and the most astute readers will notice this right out of the box as they are thumbing through the pages. Again as the book is a finely crafted piece of art it must be treated as such. A manuscript full of issues looks unprepared, unrefined, and also leaves a ding in the credibility of the author.

**Issue 7: Long Narrative Rants by Characters:**
Ok we get it, your main character does not like fill in the blank, pollution, terrorism, abortion, or the color of the walls. However, the place for characters to express long diatribes and soap boxes of information is not inside the text of the book. The reader really does not care about the political views of the character if they are not relevant to the story. Unless the book is politically based or it is important to the story these elements have no place here.

**Issue 8: Lack of Tension:** Many authors largest mistake is not giving an adequate level of tension between characters and leaving a lot of development off the table. This means that the reader has no way to buy into the plot line that the writer is executing without the proper level of conflict. Without the reader buy in, most likely the book will be folded, closed, and set to the side.

**Issue 9: Lackluster Writing:** So people come to books to have an experience and to escape the everyday and mundane existence which plagues us. For this reason the quality of writing, style, verse, prose, and every line should be high above the content which is being read in the daily paper. The content must transport, lift and inspire. Many writers forget this in their style and instead continue with the same writing they might utilize while writing a memo or something of that sort. Readers do not buy content for lackluster content so as writers we must remember our fundamental role as guides on a journey which we are leading.

**Issue 10: Riddled with Clichés:** What is a cliché exactly? It is a tired notion that has become a part of a piece of literature. It can be a person; it can be an example, a theme, or a setting. Clichés are not isolated only to people. It could be the image of the damsel in distress who is unable to do anything on her own or it could be the 50s greaser.

Readers are looking for new people, new places, and new devices to take them there. Considering so many ideas are merely repeated over and over the way to keep things fresh and interesting as a writer is to make certain that you are using new ways to express ideas and new ways to express people.

**Issue 11: Impatience with a Critic:** Remember when people are reading your work before it is submitted for publishing that they may be critical of certain elements. A friend who reads your work may not give you an honest opinion of your work and may offer you an inflated idea of the quality. Make certain that before your manuscript is submitted for publishing that it is completely edited, not just for content but for style, clichés and any other lurking issues.

**Issue 12: Egos:** Writers out there, this kind of fits into the previous issue that I've just discussed but let's be honest, as writers we all have a bit of an ego, and would like to believe that excellent content can be produced on the first version without revision and editing. However, we must remember that we are perfectly able to improve our work. And sometimes it takes an outside perspective to know how and where to improve.

Little details are sometimes glossed over in a manuscript review when we are looking at it ourselves. Again it is best to have a manuscript undergo at least 3 revisions before it is uploaded to kindle as final content. When unfinished or flawed copy is presented to readers the brand of the writer is ultimately what is cheapened.

**Issue 13: Curse of Knowing:** This is a disease which writer's suffer from which means that they have a hard time expressing what it is they are trying to say. Considering the writer knows the entire plot, all of the characters and everything that he wants to transfer to the paper it is easy to see how some of the transfer of knowledge could be missing. Essentially as writers it is very important for us to remember that people cannot read our minds and will not know what it is we are trying to say, that is unless we write it.

**Issue 14: Talking Down to Readers:** For a writer it is very important for him to remember that his readers are his flock. Therefore, a writer should write like a teacher to impart information and to share knowledge. The worst thing possible that a writer can do to isolate the audience is to decide that he needs to speak from a pulpit and talk down to the readers.

**Issue 15: Just Like Everyone Else:** Make certain that your manuscript is not the same as everyone else's, make it unique. Find out what books and other works are already on the market that are similar to yours. Research to make sure that you are not copying intentionally the same plot line, setting or the same character models over and over again, this way your work will be unique and more likely to sell.

In summation make certain that you avoid these pitfalls and know what works and what doesn't work. Your manuscript should undergo at least 2-3 revisions before it is uploaded and the more critical the eye looking at your work the better. This will help you avoid mistakes that will leave you dead in the water and wondering what happened.

## Chapter VIII: A Perfect Beginning and Perfect End

In a book what makes a great beginning? How do you grab your reader and keep them there?

### Great Book Beginning Elements:

**Great Character Development:** The first thing that a reader will start to connect with in the book will be the character. Is he real? Is he able to connect with the reader? Does the reader have an invested stake in the first few pages with the character? This all depends on the development skills of the author.

**Conflict:** There needs to be a conflict or at least the start of one. This is the way that a struggle is started whether it is a psychological struggle or a personal one. Or it might be a conflict between two opposing parties; here we must understand the intricacies of building conflict and tension. There needs to be something lurking in the beginning which is troubling the main character.

**Specific Details:** There needs to be the use of specific details in the beginning of the book so that it is possible for the reader to connect with the setting, the location, the dialect, and all other attributes. The reader will easily be able to connect to the location which is being used and will also be able to feel as if they are in the shoes of the character.

**Style:** Here you as the author have to be the guide, there should be something universal about the tone as you open. It must be a call to the universal and a call to witness struggle and tension. As you write think about the writings of novels and books in the same category in which you are writing which are universal classics.

Following this model implement and choose the best elements of the writing styles you have read and admired. By picking elements of successful styles you are learning to be a wordsmith, and as you learn you are also able to take your craft and to use the best elements of all practices.

Also make certain that you have a friend who has a critical eye read and tell you about the beginning of the book. The first paragraph will make or break the rest of the content for the reader. The first 100 words will aid or destroy your work.

And yet do not allow those first 100 words to stop you from writing. Use your friends and those around you to assist with the critique to make you a better writer. A blinking cursor is definitely not a winning element. Sometimes fear of not writing a perfect beginning will keep a writer from starting.

Many set off to write the great American novel and then find themselves stifled by the first sentence. Do not find yourself as one of those people who is stifled by fear of failure, be open to criticism and grow and learn as a writer.

## Engaging Middle Context

No part of a book should be considered downtime. Make certain that just because you are in the middle of the book you are not taking a break in the devices of great plot development. Follow your outline and make certain that you are using all of the winning elements of design.

## An Amazing Conclusion

What makes an amazing ending is a slightly subjective experience for the reader, some want enlightenment, some want inspiration, some want to learn, some want truth. However, the most important thing here is the ending is partially the take away and partially the last thought.

**Tie up Loose Ends:** For a reader who invests time in a story, knowing what happened to the main characters in the end is pivotal. Unless there is a second and third book which are waiting in the wings this must be done. Think back to watching the last episode of the Sopranos, every person who has seen the finale episode leaves the series wondering what happened to all parties involved. The simple fade to black ending leaves the mind wondering, questioning, and somehow without fulfillment.

When you invest the time to read a book each person gains a personal interest in the characters this means that there is a direct relationship between the character and the reader. When you are psychologically invested in this way it is impossible not to worry about the outcome for the character and his interests. In this respect of your reader unless you are planning a sequel please ensure that you plan the details of the tie up.

What does this mean? There should be nothing left to circumstance as to where the characters went or what they did. We should know 100% how things ended.

**Happy Ending:** In a perfect world everyone gets what they want, some readers will always find this to be the most satisfying ending in which all parties have their way and everyone moves forward in the way they wish. Readers identify with this sort of ending somewhere psychologically as it is able to take them back to times when things were "simpler". Imagine for example the parent reading to the child in bed who is sitting there intently awaiting the outcome for those few final golden words, "And they lived happily ever after." This can be a huge determining factor in the success or failure of a manuscript if the ending does not harken back to those childhood days if this is the message the writer is trying to induce.

**Informational or Informative Ending:** This ending should be one that educates the reader and tells them something that they did not know before whether it is about life, experience, culture or something that is outside of the ordinary. An example of this sort of writing brought to mind is that of Kate Chopin's the *Awakening*, although it was written in the early 1900s, this book is an amazing statement about life as a kept woman. The main female character finds herself, dressed in the best clothes, in the best house, like a caged bird full of expectations. She rejects her expectations and eventually departs in suicide. At the end of the book the reader is left grasped by shock at her perspective and education on the Victorian female perspective.

**Endings that Anger:** These usually include arbitrary endings and arbitrary violence to the character or to someone who is pivotal to the story. Some elements of this might include the immediate death of one of the very key characters who it is unthinkable to lose, or it might also involve an act of violence against key characters. Other elements include ending plots which seem to come from nowhere, strange design elements which have nothing to do with the rest of the story or are in complete contempt of the writing style and expectation of the author.

With all that said the next question many ask is why would anyone write this way? One of the best elements of good writing as well as one of the best elements of good design is the element of surprise. If you are left on the edge of your seat throughout the course of a book dying to see what will happen next and then when you finally, as a reader get to the end of the book only to see that the time investment you have made ends abruptly.

As a writer do not be surprised if the ending changes and is modified as you go along. This is one of the elements of good book and plot design as this means that you are growing as a writer and that you are planning an intriguing book. The most important thing as a writer is to remember that the beginning is an amazing start and you want to make your reader be engaged, committed, and invested to the character and to the story.

In the middle of the book make certain that there is never a down or sleepy moment, whether in plot or dialogue. And lastly give your reader an ending which is deserving of the characters. Do not cheat your readers with an ending which fades to black and does not give them an accurate idea of what is happening or what happens to the characters.

If you are writing a book with a sequel give the readers a note at the bottom that says something like To Be Continued. And consider adding a small message at the end of the book saying when you anticipate the sequel coming out. Because at that point the reader will be left hanging and hungry for more, please be considerate of their desire to know the next part of the story.

**In Summation:**

I. **An amazing beginning which engages the reader**
II. **A middle with no down time**
III. **An ending worthy of the reader's time investment.**

Hopefully this gives you an idea of how to plan the beginning, middle, and end and helps you structure your plot and time line with amazing accuracy, exaction and facilitation.

## Chapter IX: Promoting Marketing and Selling Your Kindle Book

### The Description of The Kindle Book

There are over 1100 new books which hit Kindle each day. For this reason when it becomes time to enter the description of the book you absolutely must utilize all of the resources you have. There are 4000 characters there they should all be utilized. The text must be fresh, engaging, unique and appealing to the eyes when it is first glanced at by the reader.

Also you should make certain to check out the other descriptions of books which are similar to yours in the catalogue and look at the implementation and ways they have crafted their descriptions. Firstly as you are thinking about this make certain that you are looking at award winning books in the same category.

Research the other books on the market which are competitors with yours. For example, look at the way that they used the description on Amazon and determine the best elements. After this write a list of those best elements and also of the areas of improvement. When writing your own please make certain to avoid the foibles in the description, but make certain to incorporate the winning elements.

### Steps to an Amazing Description:

1. **Research Other Books in the Same Category.**
2. **Find Award Winning Books.**
3. **Download the Full Description for the best book.**
4. **Rewrite it.**
5. **Write Your Description.**
6. **Put it Away, and then Complete Final Rewrite.**

## Your Selling Niche

Who are you targeting and selling to in marketing and planning the book? What other books which were written in the same or in a similar field are out there and how much cross over is there between your book and theirs? Who makes up the audience of those books and who are those authors targeting?

Make certain that you know who your audience is before you begin to write your description, words specifically targeted to that age group will enhance the connection that the reader has to the style of the author. Also what other books do you have that you might want to showcase in the last two paragraphs of the back of the book. Do you have 5 other books out there that are similar in subject matter to the one you are publishing? If that is the case utilize the second portion of the description to let your readers know.

When planning your books what expertise do you have in your professional life that can be added to the description to add to the validity and credibility of your pitch? Do you offer a consulting business in a particular field, let the readers know that. At the end of the book add an area for consultation contact information. And remember that one thing that a reader wants more than anything is to be able to reach out to their authors and be a part of the discussion. List your website and consultation links.

### Writing a Non Fiction Description for your Book

Want a great description? Answer these Questions

- Do you have immediate connection with the reader?
- Does it make an emotional connection?
- What is the reader's solution from all of this?
- What problems are being solved by the book?
- Does the reader know the exact benefits of the book?
- Testimonials Listed?
- Are all the details taken care of to grab all attention possible?

### Writing an Amazing Fiction Description

Fiction must be more engaging and powerful in its wording than nonfiction. Instead of selling the reader on solving a problem you are getting them to buy into the fact that they must know your story.

If you are writing a horror novel use descriptive words for fear, if it is suspense use action packed adjectives, and if it is erotica stick with words like steamy. What are some awesome examples? Here is a fun and intriguing list.

- Breath Taking
- Exciting
- Chilling
- Blood Lust
- Lusty
- Intoxicating
- Gorgeous
- Awesome
- Savage
- Fantastic
- Awesome
- Magnificent
- Arty
- Nouveaux
- Accelerated
- Suspenseful
- Frightening
- Terrifying
- Exhibitionism
- Heady
- Eccentric
- Eclectic

- Fun
- Uplifting
- Inspirational
- Randy
- Awe Inspiring
- Ambitious
- Lofty
- Uncommon

## Strap Line Power and Potential Log Line Power

When you open a book you should know in 30 seconds if you want to read it. When you open a script you will know by reading the first three lines if you would pay bucks to see it on the screen. A strap line is no exception. This is the opening line of your book and your description. It is the foundation of all of the content which is to come and you must sell your reader on their willingness to buy into that book as soon as they read the first few lines. Amazing lines such as Charles Dickens:

"It was the best of times; it was the worst of times."

In the readers mind this immediately creates a dichotomy which confuses, engages, and makes the reader need to know more from the author. How can it be both the best and the worst at the same time? This kind of amazing strapline will get the reader excited.

If you are thinking long term about taking this to the screen your strapline may become your logline. A logline is a statement that describes the entire plot in one sentence. If you do not become a wonderful wordsmith now it will be very hard to get the long term attention of a director.

### Bring Those Characters To Life

Here in the description you must bring the character to life right away and it must be done in a way to invest the reader in the story and future of the character. Who is your character? What difficult situation do they find themselves in? What is the struggle here? All of this should be written out here clearly.

### Leave Them Hanging...

Leave the reader looking at the end of the description asking, what the heck is happening here? They should be wondering what can happen next and what they can do to move forward and find out more information. They should have a hunger and curiosity to know what the next challenge will be and the next scenario.

### How do you Promote Your Ebook?

Here is a list of places where authors can promote their work for free:

YouTube: Create personal videos about the content of your book and tell the story of how it became a book.

Facebook: Start an author page for yourself, and then start a page for your book.

Authr.com: Set up a personal author page and tell others about your work.

Wordpress.com: Start a blog and share inspirations daily with your readers.

Absolutewrite.com: Communicate with other authors and advertise for free, use your own page as well as a profile.

Bookdaily.com: They have a mailing list of over 500,000 people.

Addicted to eBooks: This site allows the author to share the context of the book with the readers and share their history with the readers.

AskDavid: They have a unique marketing platform that you can utilize in the promotion of your book.

Author Marketing Club: They allow you to fill out informational forms with the implementation of widgets. Fill out one form and see your book promoted for free on multiple sites.

Bargain eBook Hunter: Offers a free form to be downloaded for promotion on Amazon and other like websites, the cover of the book is advertised along with a snippet of the content.

Books on The Knob: This site places advertising snippets on ipads, kobos, kindles and other mobile devices.

Digital Book Today: Includes both free and paid options for writers looking to share their work.

eBooks Habit: Every day they highlight 20-30 free books and then also 20-50 that are low priced, they change every day for users.

eReader News Today: Features cheap Kindle books and free Kindle books.

eReader Perks: The site is for reading, ereader devices and all things reading plus tech related. Here you will find free books for Kindle. You can also promote your book as they offer reviews and author interviews.

Flurries of Words: There are many different options here. There are paid and free advertising options for digital books as long as the books are between .99 cents and 4.99 in price. This also offers great options for writers on a shoestring budget.

FreeBooksy: Here you can submit your ebook for review so that they will consider posting it as a featured book. Also there is only one simple form to fill out in order to submit.

Frugal Reader: The website offers a freebie section where authors books which are submitted are featured as a link. The only catch with this site is that the content cannot be strictly erotica.  It may contain erotica but must not be that strictly.

Free Kindle Books & Tips: There requirements are that if you are an author and would like to have your book promoted (for free) then you have to fill out and submit a form. In addition, your book **must** be free in the Amazon Kindle Store and must have an average user rating of at least 4 out of 5 stars for consideration.

 Free eBooks Daily: Will list your free ebook. Notify them when you decide to utilize your Kindle Select Program "free" days.

Free Erotica: If you have an erotica book and you have it available for free through the Kindle Select Program notify this site and they will list your book on their site.

GalleyCat Facebook Page: This site allows you to post your book in their "New Books section".

Goodkindles: This site allows you to promote your book to its users.

Indie Books List: This particular site has many options for promoting your Kindle book.

Kindle Daily Deal: A site designed by authors for authors to assist in the promotion of work.  There are over 13000 subscribers to the site who get continual information and updates on your book.

Meet Our Authors Forum: A place on Amazon where writers discuss their work, network with one another and have their own pages.

Pixel of Ink: This allows the author to list their Kindle book if it is available as a free download.

Spicy Romance: This site allows the writer to fill out a description of their book and upload a cover image for free.

## Cheap Promotion Deals:

**Facebook advertisements**, these are very effective and as you get to set the budget on your ads on a daily basis they are very effective. As an example from personal experience I was able to gain 702 likes on a daily budget of 5.00 for 3 months.  This kind of exposure is very helpful and also has people talking about it.

If you have a pen name make certain that your pen name has a Facebook page as well as a blog for others to follow, this way they are able to keep in touch.

**LinkedIn** is also another cheap resource for advertising that is able to get your work into the hands of those who might have never heard of you otherwise. LinkedIn has 50 million users and a large following as well. Ads there like Facebook are specifically targeted to fields, interests and groups.

**Google** is another wonderful alternative for cheap marketing as they will allow you like Facebook to choose your daily or monthly budget and design a custom campaign. And with Google ads you will also be assigned a specialist who will be able to assist with the design and implementation of your campaign.

**Small local newspapers**, these are a great resource as they allow an author to take out a small ad, typically starting at around $50 and going up to around $500 for full page ads. People in a geographic area love to celebrate their local resources. For this reason there is a wonderful excitement around when a new author in an area is launched and is actively doing things like holding discussions, meetings, and sharing themselves with their neighbors.

Hopefully now you have some better ideas of how to get your ideas out there and share them with the world. Surely you will be on the Kindle's Best Seller list very soon with all of this new knowledge, amazing talent, and unbridled ambition.

In addition, if you really want to put your Kindle book marketing, promotion and selling on steroids and make even more money I have book entitled **How To Promote Market And Sell Your Kindle Book:** Amazon Kindle Publishing Marketing and Promotion Guide that will show you step by step how to exactly accomplish that goal. It is available in print, audio and Kindle book format.

This amazing book is the only cutting edge book on the subject of Kindle book marketing, promotion and selling that teaches you:

- How To Understand And Master The Amazon Kindle Book Ecosystem.
- How To "Scale" Your Kindle Book So That You Can Make A Lot More Sales and Money.
- How To Effectively Use The Internet and Social Media To Promote Your Kindle Book And Brand Yourself As An Author.

You will also learn how to effectively use marketing tactics and strategies outside of the Amazon Kindle Book Ecosystem like:

- Social Media
- Virtual Book Tours
- Press Releases
- Blogging and Guest Blogging
- Internet Radio and Podcast Shows

In addition, the following jealously guarded secrets will be revealed to you:

- How to get your Kindle book to rank on the first page of Google and Amazon.

- How to sell more books by using the secret strategy of "scaling".
- How to sell the translation and foreign rights to your Kindle book.
- The secret strategy to choosing categories.
- How to get "trusted" reviews for your Kindle book.
- How to write a killer description for fiction and non-fiction Kindle books.
- How to make your description stand out with bold letters, italics, bulleted points and Amazon orange.
- How to effectively price your Kindle book.

**A Ton of Resources Are Also Included:**

- 100 fiction book review blogs
- Press release submissions sites
- Virtual book tour companies
- Companies that produce stunning book trailers
- Book trailer submission sites
- Popular forums
- Radio and Podcast shows
- Sites to Notify for KDP Select Free Days

**And Much Much more**......

## Conclusion

First of all Congratulations are due to you for becoming a published author. This is the first step towards a life of success, fulfillment and excitement. Knowing that as an independent author through Amazon's Kindle Direct Publishing program you can control, plan and market your own destiny. This in itself is a major accomplishment and should be commended. As your book begins to sell consider what elements of marketing can be used to increase your sales.

Consider as well making your book available and free for a small period of time so that people are able to gain exposure to your work and your style. Maintain and guard your brand as an author with great scrutiny. Enhance everything you can and speak about your book. Offer to come to local libraries and universities to give talks about your book. Each opportunity is a moment for the public to connect with you, your personality, brand and style.

As you move forward think about the future of your book. Do you want it to be a movie? Do you want it to be one of a series? Are you planning an audio book? All of these elements should be considered.

Welcome to your future, where you control your success, and destiny. Hopefully now you have all of the tools to be a successful and profitable independent author and all of the traditional publishing houses will vie for a part of the action only to be left out in the cold.

## Other Books By Author

How To Create A Profitable Ezine From Scratch

The Secrets Of Making $10,000 on Ebay in 30 Days

The Complete Guide To Investing in Gold And Silver: Surviving The Great Economic Depression

How To Sell Any Product Online:"Secrets of The Killer Sales Letter"

How To Make A Fortune Using The Public Domain

Creative Real Estate Investing Strategies And Tips

How to Make Money Online:"The Savvy Entrepreneur's Guide To Financial Freedom"

How to Overcome Your Self-Limiting Beliefs & Achieve Anything You Want

The Secrets of Finding The Perfect Ghostwriter For Your Book

The Creative Real Estate Marketing Equation: Motivated Sellers + Motivated Buyers = $

How To Start An Online Business With Less Than $200

How To Market Your Business Online and Offline

How To Promote Market And Sell Your Kindle Book

Search Engine Domination: The Ultimate Secrets To Increasing Your Website's Visibility And Making A Ton Of Cash